THE ROYAL NAVY AT PORTLAND
1900 ‑ 2000

by Geoffrey Carter

It is about the year 1910. As daylight fades, dreadnoughts of the Home Fleet, with attendant cruisers, lie at anchor in Portland harbour (National Maritime Museum N21644)

Author's Note

Although many photographs have been taken of ships and naval activities at Portland, no selection can encompass all that took place there in the twentieth century. In the days when the Channel, Atlantic and Home Fleets successively visited Portland, both professional and amateur photographers recorded their presence. Similarly they marked the activities of the destroyers and submarines engaged in anti-submarine training. Photographs of the Royal Navy in Portland waters in both World Wars are comparatively scarce until the arrival of US forces prior to D-day in 1944. The return of the much reduced fleet after 1945, followed by the ships of the training squadrons, is well represented in the work of the late Graham Herbert, whose daughter has kindly given permission for some of his fine studies to be reproduced. Later, after the establishment of the Flag Officer Sea Training (FOST) regime in 1958, destroyers and frigates of the Royal Navy and subsequently NATO navies as well, undertook operational training at Portland. They were photographed by staff of the Photographic Section **HMS Osprey**, with fine shots taken from the air of each ship, often at speed, and often in rough seas. But to include too many of this kind would seem repetitive. Jack Cranny has kindly loaned photographs from his own collection and advised on ships' movements during his time with the Royal Maritime Auxiliary Service (RMAS) at Portland. The staff of the Fleet Air Museum have given me notable and enthusiastic support. Thanks are due to Steve Bush of Maritime Books for his work in preparing the book for publication.

In this book little is shown of the important work carried out at the research establishments on Portland. The development of the anti-submarine helicopter and small ships' flights at the Naval Air Station would be better recorded in a separate volume. The photographs chosen, therefore, are deemed to be historically representative of the operational activities that went on at this busy and important naval base, and of the ships, famous and little known, that went about their business in its waters.

First published in the United Kingdom in 2001 by Maritime Books, Lodge Hill, Liskeard, Cornwall, PL14 4EL

Printed and bound in the United Kingdom by J.H. Haynes & Co. Ltd., Sparkford

The Royal Navy at Portland 1900 – 2000

Before the first breakwater was completed at Portland in 1872, ships of the Royal Navy had already anchored under its protection. Then, as the age of sail came to an end, steam powered vessels were able to use purpose built facilities in the harbour to take on coal. Invasion scares, and perceived threats from France and Russia, ensured that the anchorage was well used, not only for exercises, but as a war anchorage opposite the French naval arsenal at Cherbourg. In 1864, for example Lt 'Jackie' Fisher, the future First Sea Lord, then but a young gunnery lieutenant of the new iron armoured ship Warrior in Weymouth Bay, demonstrated the efficiency of his guns' crews to the great Italian patriot Giuseppe Garibaldi. Merchantmen, too, could enter designated areas of the harbour.

It was thought that the sheltered anchorage would be suitable for a permanent training ship. First came the 'wooden wall ' *Britannia* which spent only a brief period in the lee of the Isle of Portland before departing to Dartmouth. She was succeeded by the boys' training ship *Boscawen*, which was to remain in the harbour almost continuously for the rest of the 19th century. Her presence established the tradition of Portland as a training base which lasted until its final closure in 1999.

The traditional naval rivalries between Great Britain, France, Russia and to some extent the United States of America continued until the early years of the 20th century, when they were replaced by the rising threat from the High Seas Fleet of the newly unified Germany under Kaiser Wilhelm II.

Advances in naval weaponry made the existing harbour of refuge at Portland inadequate. Particularly in the narrow waters of the English Channel, the invention of the torpedo, the torpedo boat and the submarine meant that ships in the anchorage were vulnerable to attack unless the harbour was completely enclosed. This work began in 1894 with the temporary provision of a series of dolphins and nets, followed by the building of two new permanent stone breakwaters. At about the same time the Whitehead Torpedo Factory was built in the south western corner of the harbour and production began of the very weapon that had caused such anxiety. The training ship *Boscawen* remained with two old armoured frigates *Agincourt* and *Minotaur* joining her. During this period, the harbour was very busy with the presence of the Channel Squadron and later the Channel Fleet. Manoeuvres took place regularly in the harbour and at sea. They included competitions between ships in the speed of coaling, accuracy of gunnery and the hoisting in and out of anti-torpedo nets. In the Channel, gunnery practice reverberated along the Dorset coast, bringing complaints from disturbed folk ashore and inspiring Thomas Hardy's poem 'Channel Firing'. Large numbers of warships were at Portland for much of each year, and at times they assembled for a Royal Review. It was on such an occasion, in May 1912, that Lt C R Samson piloted the first aircraft to become airborne from a moving warship as the battleship *Hibernia* steamed at 10.5 knots. Then, in 1914, the last days of peace saw the assembly of the Reserve Fleet and ships that were soon to become the Grand Fleet. It was from Portland that they all sailed to their war stations.

The departure of the Grand Fleet to the North Sea and the movement of other battleships to Dover and the Nore meant a change in Portland's role. Nevertheless, to afford additional protection against torpedo attack the old battleship *Hood* was sunk across the southern entrance in November 1914. Ships still sailed into Portland waters for gunnery practice in the English Channel, and it was on such an occasion that the battleship *Formidable* was torpedoed and sunk by the German submarine *U 24*. The submarine threat throughout the war required that Portland should be one of a number of anchorages from which anti-submarine vessels of the Auxiliary Patrol could operate. It was on such a patrol that the armed yacht *Lorna* sank a U boat in West Bay in 1918. Indeed it was to anti-submarine work that the base became increasingly committed. The Fish hydrophone was tested there and, in 1917, seaplanes were accommodated on a slip in the harbour and flew on anti-submarine patrols. Weymouth and Portland formed one of the assembly points for the French coal trade, where colliers assembled to be passed through patrols to French ports. The Whitehead torpedo factory continued in production throughout the war.

In a period of economic strain following the war, the Royal Navy remained responsible for the defence of Empire trade. A series of international conferences, aimed at limiting the naval strength of the major powers, contributed to a reduction in the size of the British Fleet from its pre 1914 strength. Nevertheless, between the wars the Atlantic and later the Home Fleet continued to assemble at Portland for training and as a departure point for cruises overseas. Ships carried out gunnery exercises with both full and sub-calibre firing of main and secondary armament, including night firing. They also engaged in torpedo practice and exercised their anti-aircraft armament. Sea going gunnery training ships, notably the battle cruiser *Tiger*, were frequently present at Portland during their training programmes. The dockyard was saved from possible closure and assumed the title of a Naval Base, and **HMS Osprey** was commissioned as an anti-submarine school. Submarines, patrol vessels and destroyers exercised tactics for engaging submerged submarines. Although there was perhaps an over optimistic assessment of the effectiveness of ASDIC, the training gave valuable experience to anti-submarine officers in World War Two, notably

Commander, later Captain F J Walker. Submarines also exercised with the battle fleet. Fleet assemblies and Royal Fleet Reviews were held on several occasions in Weymouth Bay between the wars. Shore gunnery, torpedo and underwater experimental establishments were built on Portland. The approach of war in 1939 saw an assembly of the Reserve Fleet in Weymouth Bay and preparation once more for the protection of trade and cross channel troop movements against enemy attack.

Soon after war was declared, Vice Admiral Hon E R Drummond CB MVO was appointed to command Portland Naval Base, the first Flag Officer since the First World War. But as Portland was designated a sub command, he remained responsible to the Commander in Chief Portsmouth. The next six years can be divided into a defensive and an offensive phase. During the period of the 'phoney war' before the German invasion of France and the Low Countries, ships continued to work up and an examination service was established in Weymouth Bay to prevent contraband cargoes reaching Germany via the English Channel. There was some U-boat activity in the early months of the war. Degaussing methods to counter German magnetic mines were developed at Portland. The German occupation of France caused a dramatic reappraisal of the role Portland could adopt. From French airfields the German Air Force could reach Portland in about 20 minutes. The base was particularly vulnerable to air attack, this being dramatically demonstrated by the sinking of the auxiliary anti-aircraft vessel *Foylebank* in the harbour on 4 July 1940. It was during this action that Leading Seaman Jack Mantle continued to fire his guns after being mortally wounded. For his bravery he was awarded the Victoria Cross, the first to be awarded for such an act in home waters. Thereafter, the base became virtually untenable until air superiority could be restored. Channel convoys had to be maintained but were subject to attack from aircraft and German E boats. Preparations were made to defend the harbour against a German invasion.

Once Germany attacked Russia, the balance of power over the Channel changed. From 1942 offensive operations increased. A training establishment for Coastal Forces, **HMS Bee**, was commissioned at Weymouth, and an operational base, **HMS Attack**, commissioned at Portland. In 1943 the Small Scale Raiding Force carried out a number of operations overnight, putting landing parties ashore on the Normandy coast and the Channel Islands. On a larger scale preparations began for the invasion of Europe in June 1944. Weymouth and Portland became the assembly area for Force O, which was to carry US assault troops destined for Omaha Beach; the harbour and anchorage once more accommodating large numbers of ships. After the invasion, follow up convoys sailed and returned, a bombarding force sailed from Portland to shell German batteries at Cherbourg, and later the battleship *Rodney* carried out a controlled bombardment of guns on Alderney. Following D-day, German U-boats returned to the Channel and a number of losses occurred on both sides. At the end of the war three U-boats surrendered in Portland waters.

The immediate post war period was characterised by the loss of empire and reduction in the demands made upon the Royal Navy. It was also a period when the fleet was considerably reduced in size. Many of its ships were old and worn out, and the United Kingdom passed through a series of economic crises in which defence could not always demand a high priority. The big ships soon returned to Portland, some as part of a much diminished Home Fleet and others making up a Training Squadron of battleships and later aircraft carriers. A tragedy occurred in October 1948 when a launch carrying men back from shore leave was swamped on its way to the carrier *Illustrious*, 29 men being drowned. **HMS Osprey** returned to Portland and antisubmarine training there was resumed. Submarines now attained faster underwater speeds and could remain submerged for longer periods. They operated for many years from the depot ship Maidstone, and it was while alongside her that the *Sidon* suffered a torpedo explosion and was sunk. The Albert Medal was posthumously awarded to Temp. Surgeon Lt C E Rhodes whose selfless act helped to save the lives of others but cost his own. The US nuclear submarine *Nautilus* arrived at Portland after passing beneath the Arctic ice cap.

Although there were post war proposals that the base at Portland should close, its future became much more secure with the appointment of Vice Admiral W G Crawford CB DSC as the first Flag Officer Sea Training. From then until its eventual closure, the base established an international reputation for its realistic operational sea training, not only with ships of the Royal Navy, but also with those of other NATO countries. Training was always rigorous, and responded to operational experience such as the Cod Wars and the Falklands campaign. Underwater weapons establishments continued their experimental work which attracted the attention of Soviet Intelligence, leading to the Portland Spy Case. The base also assumed an important role in the development of the helicopter as an anti-submarine weapon forming part of the armoury of destroyers and frigates. As early as September 1946, Lt(A) A Bristow landed a Sikorsky R4B helicopter on a specially constructed landing deck aboard the frigate *Helmsdale*. To accommodate and operate these aircraft and their support services, land was reclaimed from part of the harbour and a major air station came into operation. Despite the success of FOST, renewed pressure on the defence budget after the end of the Cold War led to a reappraisal of its location. Furthermore, technological advances meant that more sea room was required than could be provided by the relatively narrow and shallow English Channel and the decision was taken to transfer FOST to Plymouth. **HMS Argyll**, flying the flag of the last Flag Officer Sea Training at Portland, sailed for Plymouth in July 1995, then the last Lynx helicopters transferred to Yeovilton in 1999. Thus 150 years of naval activity at the Portland base came to an end.

Geoffrey Carter

The training ship **Boscawen** (centre) first arrived in Portland Roads in 1866 and remained, apart from a brief interlude, until 1905. The original vessel was replaced by **Trafalgar** in 1873 but the name **Boscawen** was retained. As the Royal Navy grew in strength, the old armoured frigates **Minotaur** and **Agincourt** accommodated the additional cadets as **Boscawen I** and **Boscawen II**.

(Author's collection)

Boscawen's cadets engaged in sail training, crossing yards, setting up top mast rigging and weapon practice with rifles and field pieces. They also coaled ship, received lead line instruction and maintained a fire brigade. Here they demonstrate how they cleaned and scrubbed boats.

(Author's collection)

Battleships of the Majestic class, with attendant cruisers, protected only by the southern arm of the Portland breakwater. Part of the Channel Fleet, the ships were painted black, with white upper-works and buff funnels. The line of dolphins in the distance marked the temporary protection against torpedo attack until the harbour was fully enclosed . *(Author's collection)*

The Fleet assembled in Portland harbour. Nearest, across the Bincleaves torpedo pier are pre dreadnought battleships, while in the distance can be seen the distinctive tripod masts of the first of the newly built dreadnoughts. The ships were painted grey from 1904 - 1905. *(Seward/Author's collection)*

Beyond the coaling pier, battleships, battlecruisers and cruisers are assembled. Funnel markings indicate the presence of **Agamemnon**, **Lord Nelson**, **Collingwood** and **St Vincent**, as well as the light cruisers **Gloucester** and **Southampton**.

(Seward/Author's collection)

HMS Imperieuse arrived at Portland as a destroyer depot ship in 1905. Known for a time as **Sapphire II**, she reverted to her original name in 1909. She was built as an armoured cruiser in 1883 with sailing rig for economical cruising. The design was not successful, but performance was improved when the rig was removed in 1886-7. **Imperieuse** remained at Portland until October 1913.

(Author's collection).

The battleship *Triumph* at anchor with a snow covered Portland behind her. Gunnery practice was a common feature of fleet activity before 1914, and it was claimed that *Triumph's* gunfire had disturbed the peace of Dorset villages around Lulworth. The Admiralty was not sympathetic.

(Author's collection)

The enclosure of the harbour by new breakwaters in the early part of the century was the Admiralty response to the threat of attack by fast torpedo boats. To combat these, torpedo boat destroyers were built. One of the most powerful to enter service before World War One was **HMS Swift**, built in 1907 and driven by turbines that gave her a speed in excess of 40 knots. *Swift* had an active war, serving with the Dover Patrol and taking part in the Zeebrugge operation in 1918.　　　　　*(Author's collection)*

Lieut. C R Samson takes off in the Short S.38 T2 from a ramp built on the forecastle of the battleship *Hibernia* on 2 May 1912. The ship was steaming at 10.5 knots, and the event marked the first time an aircraft had taken off from a moving warship.

(Fleet Air Arm Museum)

The cruiser *Rurik* was one of a squadron of Russian warships to visit Portland before the First World War. Present at Spithead for the Royal Review in 1909, she was at Portland in September 1913. A coal burner, the ship was built by Vickers and was designed to incorporate the hard lessons learned in the Russo-Japanese war. *(Author's collection)*

The battleship *Tsarevitch* was part of a squadron of the Russian Baltic Fleet that visited Portland in September 1913. The ship had been damaged in the Russo-Japanese War before joining the Baltic Fleet. Salutes were exchanged with the British *Dreadnought*, present in the harbour.

(*Author's collection*)

As war against Germany became imminent, a test mobilisation of the fleet took place in 1914. Instead of dispersing, the ships assembled at Portland in July. At 0700 on 29 July they were ordered to their war stations. When this photograph was taken, the ships of the First Fleet (later the Grand Fleet) had already sailed. The pre dreadnought battleships of the Duncan class followed later, cheered on their way to war.

(Imperial War Museum Q102487)

When war broke out there was concern that the southern entrance exposed ships in Portland harbour to torpedo attack from torpedo boats and submarines. It was decided to sink a block-ship across the entrance and in November 1914 the old battleship **Hood** was selected. Stripped of her armament, still carrying her topmasts, but with only one of her twin funnels standing, she was scuttled, unexpectedly turning over and resting bottom up. Though slowly breaking up, she remains there to this day. *(Imperial War Museum Q102501)*.

The battleship *Formidable*, shown here at anchor in Portland harbour before the war, was the first British battleship to be sunk by torpedoes fired from a submarine. Early on New Year's Day 1915, as part of the 5th Battle Squadron, *Formidable* was the last ship sailing in line ahead when she was struck by torpedoes from **U24**. 35 officers and 512 men were lost. The Admiral commanding the squadron was held responsible by the Admiralty and ordered to haul down his flag.

(Author's collection)

The departure of the fleet into the North Sea left Portland with a minor, though still significant, role for the rest of the war. The Portland sea area became known as Area XIII and sustained auxiliary patrol vessels engaged in anti-submarine warfare in the English Channel. By 1917, aircraft had joined the anti-submarine forces at the base and remained there until the end of the war. This machine, a Short 184 N1771 taxies past the coaling pier in 1918. In May the aircraft struck a tree and force landed in a field near Budleigh Salterton, Devon.

(Fleet Air Arm Museum)

A large number of vessels requisitioned from the fishing fleets and private sources made up the Auxiliary Patrol. Here, trawlers, drifters and yachts are assembled at Portland, probably at the end of the war. Although they may have succeeded in keeping the U-boats submerged, only one was sunk by them in local waters, when the armed yacht *Lorna* sank **UB74** in Lyme Bay on 26 May 1918.

(National Maritime Museum N21647)

Towards the end of the First World War, Admiral Beatty was planning air attacks on the German Fleet in its bases. The armistice intervened and the Grand Fleet dispersed, but there remained a desire to test the effectiveness of an attack by torpedo bombers on a fleet anchorage. In September 1919 the Atlantic Fleet assembled at Portland and a practice torpedo attack was carried out on 6 September by Sopwith Cuckoo aircraft. The battleships *Queen Elizabeth*, *Malaya* and *Barham*, and the battlecruiser *Implacable* were all targets. The photograph, though of poor quality, shows the splash of a torpedo dropped from a Cuckoo just inside the breakwater, an action which presages Taranto and Pearl Harbour.

(Fleet Air Arm Museum).

Portland's major contribution between the wars was in the field of anti-submarine warfare. The old cruiser *Gibraltar*, after a brief period as depot ship for the Auxiliary Patrol at Portland, became depot ship for the newly formed anti-submarine school on 1 November 1920. She continued in this role until 1923, when her task was transferred to **HMS Heather** afloat and then **HMS Osprey** ashore. Except for a period during the Second World War, when the role transferred to Dunoon, **Osprey** remained at Portland until final closure in 1999. (*Author's collection*)

HMS P40 was part of the anti-submarine flotilla at Portland in the early 1920s. With low freeboard and shallow draught, her silhouette was not unlike that of a submarine. The type was found unsatisfactory for ASDIC work. In October 1918, Lord Louis Mountbatten was 1st Lieutenant of **P31** when she escorted the liner **Olympic** from Portland to St Helens, apparently at 23 knots, which, if true, exceeded the P boat's designed maximum speed. *(Wright & Logan)*

In 1922 the seaplane carrier **Ark Royal**, seen in the background, was engaged with the Flying Boat Development Flight, in testing the performance and seaworthiness of flying boats when operating away from shore based facilities. **Ark Royal** was accompanied by the destroyer **Tintagel**, and the tug **St Martin** was responsible for towing the RAF seaplane dock in the foreground. While the anchorage at Portland was described as very safe, the harbour was also congested for flying boats approaching or leaving their moorings. In 1935, **Ark Royal** was renamed **Pegasus**, the original name being transferred to a new, purpose built aircraft carrier, the famous **Ark Royal** of World War Two. *(Author's collection)*

The anti-submarine flotilla's old and slow patrol vessels were replaced in 1925 by the destroyers **Rowena**, **Thruster**, **Salmon** and **Torrid**. The flotilla took out classes of trainee operators from the A/S school, exercising with submarines. **Rowena** and **Salmon** are nearest the camera.

(Wright & Logan)

Submarines were present at Portland between the wars, maintained by a number of depot ships including **Vulcan, Lucia, Titania** and **Alecto**. **Vulcan** was commissioned as a submarine depot ship as early as 1909 and served in home waters until 1930. Here she is mother ship to a group of H class boats and 'anti-submarine' submarine **R4** of the 6th flotilla. **R4** was reported to be a boat 'to which things happened', including, in 1928 a collision with the destroyer **Thruster** while surfacing. *(Author's collection)*

A fine shot of **R10** with the Chequered Fort in the distance. Designed to achieve a high under water speed, these boats could reach 15 knots submerged, but they were less manageable on the surface. As hunter killer submarines they carried six 18" bow torpedo tubes. The concept was ahead of its time, limited by the lack of effective detection equipment other than the periscope. After several years service with the anti-submarine school at Portland, the boat was scrapped in 1930.   *(Author's collection)*

This photograph shows the range of ships present at Portland in the early 1920s. In the distant background are a C class cruiser, the battlecruiser **Hood** and a battleship of the **Iron Duke** class. Nearer to the camera are destroyers and their depot ship, the repair ship **Reclaim, HMS Heather** of the anti-submarine school is at her mooring, while in the destroyer pens are several PC patrol boats, **P40**, submarines of the L and H classes and, against the outside arm, several tugs.

(Author's collection)

Ships of the 1st Minesweeping Flotilla, seen alongside the Loading Pier, were based at Portland in the late 1920s and early 1930s. Of the Aberdare or Hunt class, they were the first purpose built fleet minesweepers. By 1939 most of the remaining ships of the class were in reserve but were made ready for war. Being coal burners, they were known as the 'Smokey Joes'. Nine 'Smokey Joes' arrived at Portland as the 4th Minesweeping Flotilla in the spring of 1944. They helped to recover bodies from the sea after the disaster off Slapton Sands in May (a convoy of eight Landing Ship (Tank) on a training exercise had been attacked by nine E-boats causing large loss of life) then swept a channel to Omaha Beach prior to the D day landings in June.   (Author's collection)

'**The Mighty Hood**', in her time the largest warship in the world, was a frequent visitor to Portland between the wars. During the period from 1924 until 1936, she was flagship of the Battle Cruiser Squadron of the Atlantic Fleet and later the Home Fleet. In September 1935 she was at Portland when a special signal from the CinC Home Fleet brought her to four hours notice for steam. The Blue Peter flew to recall men who were ashore, and just before midnight the ship sailed for Gibraltar, working up to a speed of 22 knots. She was on her way to reinforce the Mediterranean Fleet during the Italo-Abyssinian crisis. **Hood's** rapid destruction by the German battleship **Bismarck** in May 1941, with only three survivors, stunned the nation.

(Author's collection)

On 10 January 1924, *L24* was one of a group of submarines engaged in an exercise off Portland which included attacking the battle fleet. During the exercise, the battleship *Resolution* 'felt a slight bump' and her paravane chain parted at a depth of 32 feet. Her stem had struck the submarine which was sunk with all hands. When located, it was found that *L24's* forward hatch was open, there was damage on the starboard side and both planes were set to hard dive.

(Author's collection)

The submarine **M2** was unique in that she carried an aircraft. The machine, a Parnall Peto, was accommodated in a hangar forward of the conning tower. Built in 1920 as a monitor submarine, she first carried a 12 inch gun before the conversion to carry an aircraft in 1928. On 26 January 1932, **M2** was reported missing. The wreck was found in West Bay, to the west of Portland. It seemed that the hangar door may have been opened too soon as the submarine surfaced, or that somehow the after ballast tanks had flooded. Attempts to raise M2 failed, and in December the Admiralty decided to abandon all salvage operations.
(Author's collection)

The K class submarines had three systems of propulsion. On the surface they used steam driven turbines plus Diesel-electric engines, with battery driven electric propulsion when submerged. They were designed to work with the battle fleet and were very expensive. As designed they lacked seaworthiness, and to improve this, bulbous bows were fitted as seen in this photograph of **K 12**. The boat's two funnels are raised. This boat escaped unscathed from the 'Battle of May Island' in January 1918, being finally sold for scrap in 1926.   (*Author's collection*)

The battle cruiser *Tiger,* a fine looking ship that had been present at the Battles of the Dogger Bank and Jutland in the First World War. After the war she served with the Atlantic Fleet, colliding with the battleship *Royal Sovereign* at Portland in 1920. Between 1924 and 1926 she was frequently at Portland as sea-going gunnery firing ship. *(Seward/author's collection).*

Ships of the Home Fleet assembled in Weymouth Bay, probably for review by King George V. The newest British battleships **Nelson** and **Rodney** and the older battlecruisers **Hood** and **Renown** can be seen beyond the 'C' class light cruiser in the foreground.

(Author's collection)

H class submarines of the 6th flotilla with their depot ship *Alecto*. These submarines exercised with the fleet and the anti-submarine flotilla. By 1939 they were obsolete and were relegated to a training role except for a period in 1940/1941 when they became operational in the English Channel and the North Sea. *(Author's collection)*

The new cruiser *Glasgow* ran aground in Weymouth Bay on 20 October 1937 while exercising coming up to a buoy. Members of the ship's company were assembled aft to help get her off. *Glasgow* was refloated after about an hour.

(Author's collection)

Ships of the Home Fleet assemble at Portland in May 1939. The battleship **Nelson**, an R class battleship and the battlecruiser **Repulse** are present together with new Tribal class destroyers including **Afridi** and **Ashanti**. In May the ships escorted the King and Queen aboard the liner **Empress of Australia**, then on 1 June the destroyers were summoned urgently to attend the submarine **Thetis**, which had sunk in Liverpool Bay.

(National Maritime Museum N21693)

Royal yachts were frequent visitors to Portland and Weymouth Bay, usually to accommodate the monarch during a review of the Fleet. Here *Victoria and Albert* lies at her buoy in the bay in the 1930's. As no Royal Standard is flying, the King is not on board.

(Graham Herbert)

In early August 1939, the Reserve Fleet assembled in Weymouth Bay and was reviewed by King George VI. The CinC Reserve Fleet was Vice Admiral Sir Max Horton, later to achieve fame as the CinC Westem Approaches during the Battle of the Atlantic. Here his flag flies in the recently reconstructed cruiser *Effingham.* The ship had a brief war career, being wrecked off Norway in May 1940.

(Author's collection)

The destroyer *Grenade* exercising off Portland in December 1939. Already camouflaged, she went on to serve in the Norwegian campaign before being lost. As part of the 1st Destroyer Flotilla she was sent to reinforce ships engaged in the evacuation from Dunkirk. She was bombed and sunk just outside the harbour on 29 May 1940, close enough inshore for many survivors to swim ashore.

(National Maritime Museum MAH1)

The German occupation of the French Channel coast rendered Portland intensely vulnerable to air attack. On 4 July 1940 the auxiliary anti-aircraft ship **Foylebank** was dive bombed and sunk at her mooring in the harbour despite warning from her Type 280 radar. She is shown shortly after the attack, listing to port and on fire amidships. Leading Seaman Jack Mantle was awarded the Victoria Cross for continuing to fire the starboard pompom even though mortally wounded. The pompom is visible on a sponson below the bridge. Two other members of the ship's company were awarded the DSM.

(Author's collection)

Weymouth and Portland became important bases for Coastal Forces. Boats worked up at **HMS Bee** in Weymouth, while **HMS Attack**, commissioned in January 1941, was an operational command at Portland. Among the assembled vessels, warship spotters will recognise MTBs, MLs, a Steam Gunboat (SGB) and a TID class tug. The year is probably 1944. *(Geoffrey Hudson)*

MTB 344 was built by Thornycroft and purchased by the Admiralty in 1941. She was used by the Small Scale Raiding Force (SSRF) to carry out raids on the Channel Islands. Frequently departing from Portland at dusk, she would carry out an operation before returning to harbour early the following morning. The boat is seen here travelling at speed off the Dorset coast with commandos on board.

(Courtesy R van Riel)

The build up to D Day marked the height of naval activity at Portland during the Second World War. The United States Forces destined for Omaha beach assembled at Weymouth and Portland, and the harbour was full of transports, landing craft and British and American naval vessels. *LST 314*, seen here loading at Castletown, was sunk by a German E boat on 9 June, half her crew being lost.

(US Army)

The US **LST 75** loading alongside Castletown pier for the invasion of Normandy in June 1944. Ships loaded at Portland included 24 LST, 133 LCT, 46 LCM and 32 LCP(L).   (*Author's collection*)

To support the US Army assault on Cherbourg an Anglo-American Task Force sailed from Portland to bombard the German shore batteries there. Bombardment Group One was made up of the US battleship **Nevada**, the US cruisers **Tuscaloosa** (flag) and **Quincy**, the British cruisers **Glasgow** and **Enterprise**, and destroyers and minesweepers. The German batteries responded with accuracy, here hitting **Glasgow** in the port aircraft hangar.

(Imperial War Museum A24310)

In May 1945, three German U-Boats surrendered at Portland. *U-249* was brought into Weymouth Bay by the frigates *Amethyst* and *Magpie*, and *U-1023* surrendered the same day. Later in the month *U-776* surrendered and was escorted in by the frigates *Garlies* and *Gore*.

(*Author's collection*)

In 1946 the elderly battleships **Nelson** and **Queen Elizabeth** returned to Portland after service with the East Indies Fleet. **Nelson**, having hosted the surrender of Japanese forces in Singapore, became successively flagship of the Home Fleet, Seagoing Training Ship and flagship of the Home Fleet Training Battleships: **Queen Elizabeth** was briefly part of the Home Fleet and also employed as an accommodation ship.

(Graham Herbert)

The remaining King George V class battleships, **King Geoge V, Duke of York, Anson** and **Howe** all served at Portland after the war. **Howe,** shown here against a darkening sky, was attached to the Home Fleet Training Squadron in August 1946. **Anson** was Flagship of the Rear Admiral Training Squadron from 1946 to 1949.

(Graham Herbert)

The oiler **Black Ranger** was built in 1940, and based at Scapa Flow throughout the war. Her operational tasks included acting as escort oiler to Russian convoys. After the war she went to the Arctic with the Fishery Protection Flotilla and to the Falkland Islands. But most of her later years were spent at Portland where she was the training oiler, practising oiling at sea with ships working up. She was finally broken up in 1975. It might be said that she began the long post war tradition of service at Portland by ships of the Royal Fleet Auxiliary.

(Crown Copyright)

Portland began its long association with helicopters late in 1945. In 1946 exercises were carried out with the Fleet. Experimental work included fitting Sikorsky R4B helicopters of 771 Squadron with 'balloon bag' undercarriages.

(Author's collection)

The first landing of a helicopter on the deck of a small warship took place in September 1947. Lieut(A) A Bristow RNVR landed on a wooden platform specially fitted to the frigate **HMS Helmsdale**.

(Author's collection)

The frigate **Leeds Castle** was one of a large number of Castle class frigates that served at Portland . In 1946 they formed part of the 3rd Escort Flotilla, and later the 2nd Training Flotilla, carrying out anti-submarine training. Underwater weapon research was by then concentrated at Portland. **Leeds Castle** was the first command of the future Vice Admiral Sir Roderick MacDonald who was later appointed the first Commander Sea Training in the new FOST organisation set up at Portland in 1959. *(Author's collection)*

A close up of the frigate **Hedingham Castle** in the Floating Dock at Portland, July 1947. Several floating docks were employed at Portland. **AFD 7** served from 1914 to 1916 and from 1920 to 1940. Later **AFD 19** was at Portland from 1945 to 1956 and **AFD 26** from 1955 to 1959.

(Author's collection)

The aircraft carrier **Illustrious** was at anchor in Portland harbour when, on the night of 17 October 1948, a motor pinnace bringing libertymen back to the ship was sunk in rough weather with the loss of 29 lives. In the previous five weeks the ship had steamed 4,500 miles and carried out 911 landings on the flight deck.

(Author's collection)

Aircraft carriers also formed part of the Training Squadron. Here **Victorious** watches over the Open Cutter Race in 1948. The ship joined the squadron in October 1947. Classrooms were built in the hangar, messdecks were altered and more boats were fitted for instructional purposes. In March 1950 she sailed for Portsmouth for conversion, her place in the squadron being taken by the battleship **Vanguard**.   (*Author's collection*)

The submarine depot ship **Maidstone** became a familiar sight at her mooring in the harbour. She arrived in October 1946 and remained until 1958, even serving from September 1956 to March 1958 as flagship of the Home Fleet. The submarine **Sceptre** is alongside.

(Graham Herbert)

The aircraft carrier **Vengeance** prepares to sail for Operation 'Rusty', a six week cruise in the Arctic Ocean to study the effects of extremely cold weather on men, ships and aircraft. Aircraft engaged in these successful operations in 1949 included Vampires, Firebrands, Fireflies, Sea Furies, Sea Otters, a Barracuda and a Dragonfly helicopter. **Vengeance** herself suffered a brittle-fracture in her flight deck due to the cold. She later relieved **Illustrious** as trials and training carrier before sailing on loan to the Royal Australian Navy in 1953. She was finally sold to Brazil in 1956 and renamed **Minas Gerais**.

(*Graham Herbert*)

MFV1060, carrying libertymen from the aircraft carrier ***Indefatigable***, comes alongside at Weymouth in July 1950, obviously in the days before Health and Safety legislation. *(Author's collection)*

The giant US battleship **Missouri** visited Portland in July 1952 in company with the cruisers **Macon, Des Moines** and 5 destroyers. On arrival, she saluted the flag of the CinC Home Fleet aboard the last British battleship **Vanguard** and was answered with a salute of 17 guns. Completed in 1944, it was aboard **Missouri** that the Japanese surrender took place in August 1945. The ship's long career included service in the Korean War 1950 - 1953 and the Gulf War 1990 - 1991 when, in addition to her 16 inch main battery, she also fired Tomahawk missiles.

(Author's collection)

If any vessel deserved an award for long service and good conduct at Portland, it would probably have to be the tug *Pilot* (far right). She was one of the many civilian manned auxiliary ships that supported the Royal Navy. Built in 1909, she was never out of commission apart from refits until she finally departed in 1960. Led by the tug *Security*, *Pilot* is alongside *LC 10* as the after part of the wreck of the auxiliary AA vessel *Foylebank* is lifted in 1952.

(Jack Cranny)

Phoenix Units from the Normandy Mulberry harbours were brought to Portland in 1946 to provide shelter for destroyers and submarines. In 1953 most of the units were sent to the Netherlands as sea defences against flooding. Those remaining have become listed buildings! *(Author's collection)*

In the 1950s a large area was reclaimed from the sea and a new 600 yard deep water jetty was built, named Queen's Pier or 'Q' Pier. Here, in May 1971, every berth is occupied. A Type 12 frigate lies alongside, together with the destroyer **Caprice** and the **RFA Engadine**. Inside the arm of the pier are the frigate **Undaunted**, the Netherlands destroyer **Noord Brabant** and the German destroyer **Z 2**.

(Author's photograph)

An aerial view of the alongside facilities at Portland. From the left the pier at Castletown projects towards the two remaining Phoenix Units brought back from the Normandy beaches. Extending from a reclaimed area is the post war 'Q' pier, shaped like an ice hockey stick and with three ships alongside. The large pier to the right is the Coaling Pier, an early feature of the harbour, built in the 19th century, and of importance in sustaining the coal burning ships of the Channel Fleet. It was largely built over. Within the curved approach to the coaling pier is the area that accommodated a floating dock. The three remaining jetties from the shore are the ML Jetty, the Loading Jetty and the Camber Jetty. The large apparently white roofed building on the far right is the original coaling shed, completed in the mid 19th century. *(Author's collection)*

The destroyer **Brocklesby,** exercising here with two Type 14 frigates, was the longest serving ship of the Hunt class. She saw much wartime active service in the North Sea, English Channel and the Mediterranean. After a period in reserve, she was refitted at Devonport, and joined the 2nd Training Squadron at Portland in 1952, serving as a trials vessel for variable depth sonar. She continued as an experimental and training ship until she paid off in 1963. Note the open bridge.

(Crown Copyright)

The Type 14 Blackwood class frigate **Murray** was part of the Portland based 2nd Training Squadron in the 1950s. The ships were designed for rapid construction in an emergency. They were intended to fulfil an anti-submarine role with sonar detection equipment for Limbo forward firing mortars. Gun armament was very light, never exceeding three 40 mm mounted on the bridge wings and aft. The ships were driven by a single screw.

(*Graham Herbert*)

In May 1953 the submarine **Andrew** arrived at Portland having completed a 2,500 mile voyage from Bermuda totally submerged. The Snort breathing apparatus made the voyage possible and it may well be that this was the first time a submarine had crossed the Atlantic without surfacing. *(Author's collection)*

On 17 June 1955, the salvage vessel **Barcross** uses camels to raise the submarine *Sidon*. The previous day an experimental torpedo had exploded aboard the submarine as she was about to set sail. Thirteen men were killed, including Temporary Surgeon Lt C E Rhodes, who was posthumously awarded the Albert Medal for his selfless acts in helping to save lives.   (*Graham Herbert*)

Navy Days at Portland in 1955 included a mock attack by X craft. The midget submarine *Stickleback* (X 51) could carry limpet mines and side charges. When submerged, a diver would be released to attach explosive charges to the chosen target. This particular boat was sold to the Swedish Navy in 1958 and renamed *Spiggen*, the Swedish crews being trained at Portland. In 1977 she was returned to Britain for preservation and can be seen as part of the Imperial War Museum collection. *(Author's collection)*

As the Royal Navy submarine *Sleuth* departs on exercises, so the US nuclear submarine *Nautilus* arrives. On her first visit in 1957, *Nautilus* was not allowed alongside, but moored in the harbour alongside the depot ship **USS Fulton**. Earl Mountbatten, the First Sea Lord, and Duncan Sandys, the Minister of Defence, visited the nuclear powered submarine.   *(Graham Herbert)*

A close up of **USS Nautilus** in 1958 as she approaches the coaling pier at Portland to a rousing welcome. It was 10 August and the submarine had just completed a voyage from Honolulu during which she passed submerged under the North Pole. Civil dignitaries were present together with a Royal Marine band and a Royal Navy guard of honour.

(Author's collection)

The British destroyer *Sluys* was first commissioned in 1946 and served with the Home Fleet, when she visited Portland. She was sold to Iran in January 1967 and renamed *Artemiz*. She achieved a moment of notoriety by running aground in the harbour on 12 February 1970.

(*Crown Copyright*)

At sea off Portland Bill in 1970, the Type 14 frigate *Exmouth* carried out trials of the new gas turbine propulsion system. Conversion was carried out between 1966 and 1968, a stream-lined funnel being set further aft after tests. She served with the Second Frigate Squadron until December 1976. *(Crown Copyright)*

During the 1970s, ships moored fore and aft in Newtons Cove, just outside the breakwater of Portland Harbour. There they carried out practice firing of anti-submarine mortars, aiming at a target ahead of the ship. Here the frigate **Mermaid** has fired her missiles, one of which can be seen high above the ship's radar. These activities were likely to startle yachtsmen emerging unsuspecting through the north entrance! **Mermaid** only served for five years with the Royal Navy. She was originally ordered by the Republic of Ghana, but was too expensive for that country and was purchased by the British Government. She served in the Far East before being transferred to the Malaysian Navy in 1977. *(Author's photograph)*

The frigate **Undaunted** as leader of the Second Frigate Squadron. A veteran of the Normandy landings, on D Day +2 she carried General Eisenhower and Admiral Sir Bertram Ramsey on a tour of the beaches. She also served with the East Indies Fleet. In 1952 she was converted into an anti-submarine frigate. At Portland in the 1960s and 1970s, much of her time was spent as a 'Channel Runner'. Fitted with a helicopter landing deck, visible in the photograph, she carried out trials with the prototype P 531 helicopter, subsequently developed and ordered as the Westland Wasp. She paid off in 1974 and was finally sunk as a target off Gibraltar in 1978.

(Crown Copyright)

The cruiser **HMS Blake** at her mooring on 29 June 1971. Her work up serials included carrying out famine relief exercises. The final configuration of the ship can be seen here, with her after 6 inch gun turret replaced by a hangar and flight deck, enabling her to operate four Wessex 3 and later Sea King helicopters, but destroying her original fine lines. The presence of the helicopters gave the ship a powerful anti-submarine capability and she was able to act as a command ship on global deployments. When **Blake** finally paid off in December 1979, she was the last true cruiser to serve in the Royal Navy.

(Author's collection)

The Royal Navy at Portland was well served by auxiliary vessels manned by civilians. They were operated by departments in the base until 1959 when they were brought under one authority, the Port Auxiliary Service. A further reorganisation took place in 1976 with the formation of the RMAS (Royal Maritime Auxiliary Service). In this photograph the tug **Capable** heads out to sea for another days exercises.

(Author's collection)

The Type 15 frigate **Verulam**, built as a destroyer in 1952, pays off at Portland in January 1971. She served as an anti-submarine trials vessel, had her 4 inch gun removed and an additional deckhouse added. She is escorted by vessels of the PAS (Port Auxiliary Service). *(Crown Copyright)*

The Battle class destroyer **Matapan** had an unusual history. Completed in 1947, she was laid up after trials until 1968, when she was brought out of reserve to become a sonar trials ship. She was commissioned in 1973 with a unique profile. She carried no weapons, but sported a raked and flared bow, a forecastle deck that extended aft and a landing deck to enable a helicopter to deliver men and equipment to the ship. A second funnel was added which housed exhausts for the diesel generators needed to power the sonar equipment. At Portland **Matapan** joined the 2nd Frigate Squadron. She was finally laid up in 1978.

(Crown Copyright)

The helicopter station at Portland opened in April 1959 as an integral part of **HMS Osprey**. The original canteen building of 1901 was converted into an administration building surmounted by the control tower. A tidal area known as The Mere was reclaimed as the requirements of the air station increased. *(Author's collection)*

Portland Navy Days were popular occasions from the 1950s to the 1980s. Normally held in July, they attracted large crowds of local people and holiday makers. Here, in 1970, a Wessex HAS Mk1 helicopter of 771 Squadron hovers before an enthusiastic audience. Behind them is the guided missile destroyer *Norfolk*, while in front can be seen two 'A' class patrol submarines. In later years, with the development of the helicopter base at **HMS Osprey,** there could be up to two hours of air display by modern and vintage aircraft in addition to the assembled ships and events held in an arena in the base.

(Author's collection)

The fast patrol boat **Cutlass** leaves Portland at speed. She was one of three vessels employed as fast attack boats during the Thursday War, a weekly large scale exercise designed to test the disciplines learned by the ships which were engaged in training at Portland. They simulated an attack by fast missile carrying craft that could threaten major warships. One of these boats was present at Portland Navy Days, demonstrating their power by a high speed run across the harbour.

(Author's collection)

It was the time of the Cod War against Icelandic gunboats in the mid seventies. This photograph was taken from the tug **Confiance**, acting as a British trawler. The frigate **Lincoln**, working up off Portland, was fitted with wooden bow sheathing to enable her to engage the gunboats at close quarters. Here she was attempting to prevent the 'Icelandic' **Sabre** from cutting the 'trawler's' nets. It looks like a near miss all round !

(Jack Cranny)

HMS _Hermes_ in Portland harbour in March 1977. Converted from a fleet aircraft carrier between 1971 and 1973 into an amphibious assault ship, she was also able to operate in an anti-submarine role with Wessex and Sea King helicopters. She was not yet fitted with the ski jump that made her so recognisable during the Falklands War of 1982. The RMAS tender **_Dunster_** is alongside.

(Author's collection)

The Royal Fleet Auxiliary *Engadine* was another regular visitor to Portland. She was a helicopter support ship, specially designed to meet the requirements of naval training in the flying, handling and maintenance of helicopters at sea.

(Author's collection)

Portland Naval Base was particularly busy during the Falklands campaign. Both merchant and naval vessels passed through FOST programmes before making the long voyage south. In this post Falklands war photograph, a Type 42 destroyer, probably **HMS Newcastle**, wearing a vertical stripe on her funnel and hull to distinguish her from Argentine Type 42s, was working up at Portland prior to deploying to the South Atlantic. The black boot topping was already beginning to show through the hastily applied grey paint. *(Author's photograph)*

As part of her operational sea training, the frigate *Jupiter* approaches the **RFA Green Rover** on 1 March 1984. She is about to take on fuel from astern . Members of the ship's company stand by under the watchful eyes of Sea Riders who are part of the FOST organisation.

(Author's photograph)

In January 1986 the 7000 ton Libyan freighter **Ebn Majid** caught fire in Portland harbour. The fire was fought by the Dorset Fire Brigade and for a time, the RMAS salvage vessel **Kinbrace** and the tug **Rollicker** lay alongside. The Dog class tugs **Basset**, **Sheepdog** and **Alsation** were also involved. The burning ship was eventually beached. In this photograph a Lynx helicopter from **HMS Osprey** hovers over the drifting smoke.

(Author's collection)

A Sea King Mk IV helicopter with the Flag Officer Sea Training aboard approaches **HMS London** during BOST (Basic Operational Sea Training) in 1988. The Captain of **HMS Osprey** at the time was Captain Chris Craig CB DSC who became Commodore of the British naval contingent in the Gulf in 1990/91. **London** was his command ship. Captain Craig was in a unique position to observe the effectiveness of operational sea training at Portland, having already commanded the frigate **Alacrity** in the Falklands campaign. *(Crown Copyright)*

The Admiralty Research Establishment acoustic calibration vessel **Crystal** lies at its mooring close to the outer breakwater. Built to test new sonar equipment, it had no propulsion unit of its own. She was sold in 1992 to a Dutch concern and was towed to Rotterdam. Portland had a long association with underwater weapon research. *(Crown Copyright)*

On Friday 21 July 1995, Rear Admiral John Tolhurst, Flag Officer Sea Training at Portland, hauled down his flag ashore for the last time and embarked in the Type 23 frigate **HMS Argyll**. His departure to set up the sea training organisation at Plymouth was low key, his ship being escorted by tugs, safety vessels and the Weymouth lifeboat. Here the escorts turn back as **Argyll** headed for the east entrance. The only naval vessel remaining in the harbour was the ex-Maintenance Ship **Rame Head**, which had been used as a training ship by the Royal Marines and the Special Boat Squadron.

(Crown Copyright)

Rame Head, previously a maintenance vessel, remained at Portland after the departure of the Flag Officer Sea Training. Moored unobtrusively in the harbour, she was used for training by the Royal Marines and the Special Boat Service. In this photograph, taken in 1992, two Sea King helicopters and a Lynx were exercising Royal Marines in rapid boarding. *(Jack Cranny)*

Before it finally closed down, **HMS Osprey** celebrated Forty Years of Naval Aviation at the Royal Naval Air Station, Portland with an Open Day on 17 October 1998. Some of the helicopters based at Portland over that period were paraded before the public. From left to right are a Wessex HAS Mk3, a Whirlwind HAS Mk7, a Whirlwind HAR Mk3, a Dragonfly HR1, and in the foreground P531, the prototype of the production Wasp. Airborne in the background is a Lynx.

(Crown Copyright)

The end of an era, Captain John Harvey salutes as the white ensign is lowered for the last time at **HMS Osprey** during the closing down ceremony, 31 March 1999. *(Fleet Air Arm Museum)*

Index of Ship's Names